C.

Elland
in old picture postcards

by Catherine Audrey Law

European Library ZALTBOMMEL/THE NETHERLANDS

Cover Picture:
Postcard of 1889 – selected areas of Elland.

Acknowledgements
I would like to thank the members of The Greater Elland Historical Society in assisting with the loan of many of the pictures included. Also, Mrs. E. Lumb, for the loan of picture number 76.
The majority of the photographs were taken at the turn of the century, by Mr. Albert Townsend, to whom we must be grateful for recording the way of life in Elland.

GB ISBN 90 288 2349 2 / CIP

© 1983 European Library – Zaltbommel/The Netherlands

Second edition, 1995: reprint of the original edition of 1983.

INTRODUCTION

The contents of this book are intended to portray, how Elland appeared during the 1880's and early 1900's. At the turn of each page, the reader should develop great enthusiasm, for there have been so many memories captured within each picture.

Elland is situated on the main route between Huddersfield and Halifax, in West Yorkshire. The name of the town means 'land by water'. Dating back to 1317, Elland was granted a charter, to hold a market, on a weekly basis, and two fairs annually. Within the town, two listed buildings of special interest. One being the fifteenth century New Hall, whilst the other is the twelfth century church of Saint Mary.

Our town is recorded in the Doomsday Book. Together with the eerie ghost stories, and the true recording of the Elland Feud, which resulted in a physical battle between two families, the town is well worth recognition. Due to the fact that the township of Elland consisted of several woollen mills, the River Calder, flowing through Elland, was a valuable necessity to the manufacturers.

Another industry, which was very much to the fore, was hand-loom weaving. This work was carried out in the local cottages, and was an ideal occupation for the family. Usually, the man of the house carried out the job of weaving, whilst his wife participated in the yarn spinning.

Although many of the properties outlined in the following pages no longer remain, it is pleasing to note that buildings which have survived the changes during the past few years, are well preserved. No doubt, they were constructed of sturdy building materials.

Prior to 1974, Elland was included within the Urban District Council. However, on April 1st of that year, local government reorganisation took place, thus the town became a section of Calderdale Metropolitan Borough Council. A census carried out during 1981, revealed that Elland had a population of 18,011.

The town is twinned with a French town, namely, Riorges. Exchange visits have been made by both parties, on several occasions, whereby pleasing results have been established.

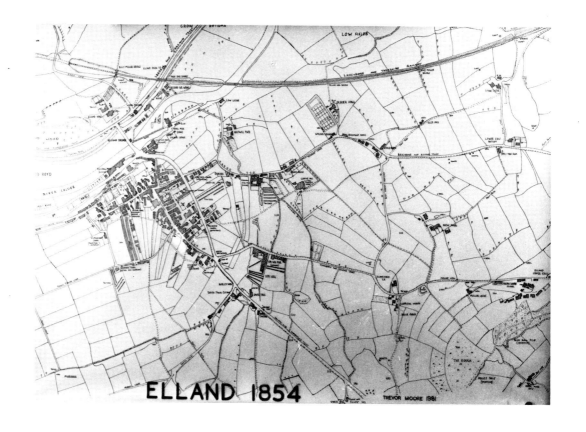

ELLAND 1854

TREVOR MOORE 1981

1. This excellent map, drawn by Mr. Trevor Moore, indicates how Elland appeared in 1854. Such changes have taken place, although many names of streets and houses are familiar. A present day map would reveal all the major developments.

2. At the junction of Coronation Street and Southgate, we can see here a vital business. Namely, Cooper Kitchen, the ironmonger. The display of wares indicates that an ample variety of goods were available. Items ranging from clothes baskets, joinery tools, and gardening implements, to name but a few. Fortunately, after more than a century of trading, the shop still offers an excellent service to present day shoppers, and deals in similar commodities. The detached house, shown further along the street, was the home of Doctor Holton during the early 1900's.

3. Further along Southgate, we have proof that these buildings have contended the re-development programme of the town. This picture having been recorded at the turn of the century. The majority of properties within the centre of this view no longer exist. Properties in the foreground are occupied nowadays by various retailers. Ranging from a tobacconist, furnishers and frozen foods dealers.

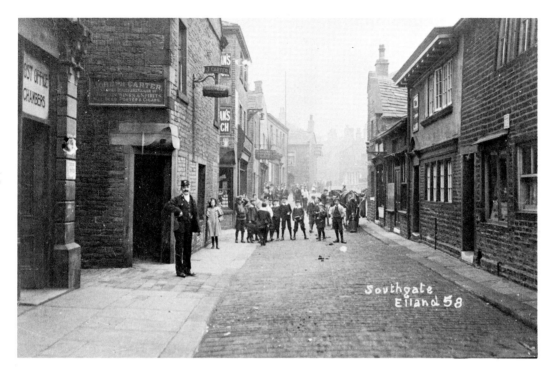

Southgate
Elland 58

4. A step back in time again reveals another section of Southgate, which has since undergone drastic demolition. To the left of this picture, the original Post Office Chambers can be seen. Directly across the pathway, the Blue Barrel Inn is highlighted. Then owned by Mr. Joseph Carter, and well known to accommodate Elland mill owners, in a special room, known as the 'House of Lords'. Prior to being destroyed, in order to make way for the 'new' Elland, the houses, as situated to the right of the photograph, had been converted into shops. A glimpse of the Royal George can be seen. This public house closed in 1912.

5. Pictured above, is a glimpse of a more updated version of Southgate, as opposed to those already shown. To the left, at the junction of Timber Street and Southgate, the Post Office can be seen. The original Post Office, in years gone by, was the responsibility of two elderly ladies. They both shared the work, one acting as postmistress, whilst the other delivered mail within the area.

6. Another section of Southgate, recorded prior to 1900. It is interesting to see that roof repairs were being expedited, to a property within the area. This gives cause, to wonder precisely what the rate of pay may have been at that time. This view also casts a degree of light upon the Yorkshire setts, which have now been replaced by tarmacadam. Although, adding to a more comfortable journey, the character of the streets has been destroyed by such an invention. A poster on the gable end of the shop reads 'SACRED CONCERT' — the date is 1904.

7. Attention is drawn to a shop named the Central Bazaar, Southgate, to the right of the picture. The name can be seen immediately above the vast window. A whole range of wares were available at this local shop. Household requisites, shopping baskets, pegs and candles and most of all, toys. This shop gave so much pleasure to children, for they could spend their weekly pocket money here. A bazaar whose name still lingers on today.

8. The gas lamp, protruding from a bracket, on the above building, at Southgate, claims much attention. In those days, it was a common sight to watch a locally appointed gentleman, lighting the gas lamps, which were present in the thoroughfares, when the dusk of night came.

9. This was how Timber Street could be seen, when Danesbury House existed. Sadly, in 1881, the property was demolished, making way for new buildings.

10. This quaint street, near St. Mary's Church, is seen here. Northgate is the area showing the Rose and Crown Inn (to the right), having ceased business in December 1914. In the background the top of Church Street can be recognised.

11. The Cross, featured here, was towards the end of Southgate, close to St. Mary's Church. A very old family business can be seen within the row of shops. For Manchester House was a well established drapers shop, owned by the Forrest family. Messrs. Swale traded in the grocery concern, next door, whilst pet foods could be obtained from the adjoining shop. The property below the pet supplies is Lloyds Bank.

12. St. Mary's Church dates back to the twelfth century, and claims much attention, justified by its position on a high plateau. The building, constructed of local stone, was erected by local craftsmen. Shown here, outside the church, is the Verger, Mr. Harry Johnson.

ELLAND PARISH CHURCH

13. The interior of St. Mary's Church consists of several architectural features. It is understood that there is a simularity between St. Mary's Church and Kirkstall Abbey. In all probability, following completion of the building of the abbey, during 1170, the masons were appointed to expedite the structure of St. Mary's Church. A highlight within this splendid building is the colourful window, to the east. Erected during the fifteenth century, it displays many of the events during the life of the Blessed Virgin Mary.

14. At the junction of Southgate and Victoria Road, a memorable sight is recorded above. The year is 1915. Hundreds of soldiers marched through the town, prior to leaving for the French battlefields. Sadly, for some it was the last time they would see their families and friends.

15. Here we can see Victoria Road, recorded before the tramlines were laid. The wooden huts, shown in between the stone buildings to the left of the view, were used as shops. At the turn of the century, Mr. Albert Townsend, a local photographer, conducted his affairs from one of the huts.

16. In order that a tram service could be introduced, work commenced on the necessary preparations. Therefore, in 1914, tram lines were laid. The labourers shown above are working on the section towards the bottom of Victoria Road, near Lowfield House.

Opening of Tramway Service Huddersfield to Elland - Jan. 14. 1914.

17. January 14th, 1914, was a special day, when the first tram arrived in Elland, following its journey from Huddersfield. Although the weather was uninviting, due to rain, this did not dampen the spirits of the Ellanders, and there was a great opportunity for crowds to gather, in order to receive the tram, and passengers upon the decks.

18. The first tram to arrive in West Vale from Halifax was during August 1905. Pictured here is an example of this service, at Stainland Road, close by the Shears Inn. The fare at that time was a standard amount of two pence.

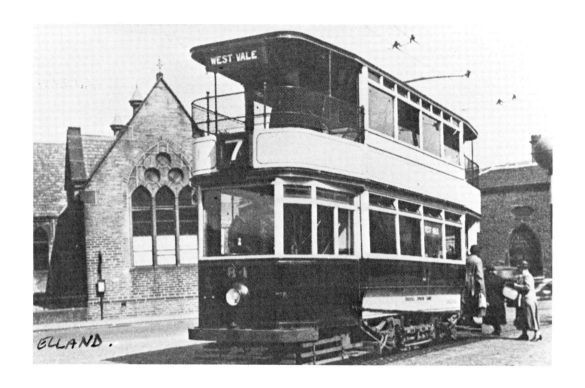

ELLAND.

19. Still on the subject of trams, in the early 1900's, the Huddersfield to West Vale service is featured here. The background scene features Elland South End School, and the Elland Prison.

20. Seen here is the 'Mexborough Arms Hotel', at the bottom of Westgate. The Landlord at that time was a Mr. C. Brier. During the 1920's the public house ceased trading.

21. These properties, at the top of Westgate, were somewhat unique in structure. Below the properties shown, the steps between the railings led to yet another dwelling. Interesting too, to note the lady using a parasol, to shade her from the sun.

22. A cross section of fashions can be seen in this feature. Flat caps and overalls, worn by the gentlemen. The women clad in long skirts and shawls, with the children dressed accordingly to those times. The local postman is yet another attraction, shown here at the top of Westgate.

23. Here we have a section of the top of Westgate, and the junction of Long Wall. A prominent and indeed notable feature is that of the tradesman at the top of the ladder. Quite a height and what an angle!

24. At the end of the 1914-1918 War, celebrations were called for. This is a section of New Street, where every effort had been made to decorate the street. The happy, smiling faces of the children reveal exactly how much pleasure they derived from the whole event.

25. From the top of Westgate, this view spans quite some distance. The building in the foreground was used for the preparation of malt. The thick woodland, to the rear of the maltings, is Elland Wood. On a pleasant summer day, families spent their leisure time there, picnicing and gathering wild bluebells.

26. A local blacksmith had two houses built, at the top of Gog Hill. When the properties were complete, he added a fascinating mark to the exterior, for there, carved within the eaves, a hammer and pincers could be identified. A section of the properties is shown above, to the right hand side of the children in the picture.

27. A gathering of youngsters is featured here, outside property at the top of Westgate, close to Gog Hill. The properties shown belonged to Joseph Smithies, and were a part of the Ellen Royde estate. Eye-catching effects are the sundial, between the bedroom windows of the cottages, and the dress style of the children. No doubt, those leather boots would have been fastened by means of a button hook. Yet another fashion of the early 1900's.

28. At the bottom of Hullen Edge Road stood the above cottages. In 1914 the tramway was extended to West Vale, therefore it was essential to demolish the above cottages. The lady, standing in the doorway of one of these properties, is Mrs. Thornton. Apparently, she had objected to vacating the premises, and she was adamant that she would reside there until such times as she was urged to surrender possession.

The Memorial, Elland.

ELD 15

29. The War Memorial stands in the park at Hullen Edge, Elland, in 6,376 acres of land. Constructed to signify the last two wars. A list of names of those unfortunate soldiers, who lost their lives during those times, is recorded on the inscription below the statue.

30. A familiar site, on the canal at Woodside, was the abundance of barges, usually they were laden with flour, which had been produced at the local flour mill. Most of the merchandise, on leaving Elland, was bound for Hull.

The Old Bridge
Elland 286

31. The pace of life, at Elland Bridge, before the bridge was widened in 1897. However, it is recorded that there was a bridge over the River Calder, at this point, as early as 1199.

32. A young lady pauses to allow the cattle seen wandering across these Yorkshire setts, to make their journey across the bridge. Evidence that the farmyard was close by.

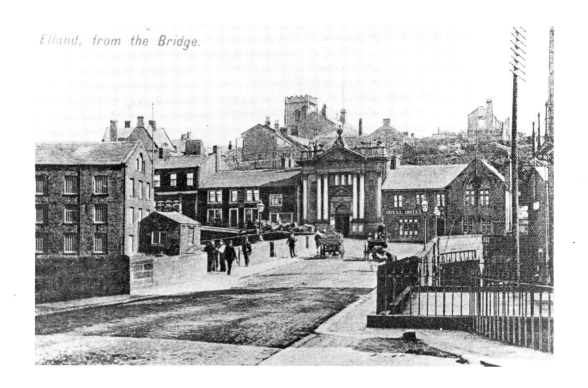

Elland, from the Bridge.

33. Briggate is the area seen from this angle of Elland Bridge. The fine structure of the Britannia Building is visible, nestled between the Royal Hotel and the Malt Shovel Inn. The pillars, constructed of 'Aberdeen' granite, add to the beauty of this imposing building, which was opened in 1895. The statue of Britannia is prominently situated on the peak of the property.

34. This photograph is associated with the previous one. It indicates the type of properties which existed prior to the construction of the Britannia Building.

35. On July 11th, 1912, Elland Bridge was lined with people. King George V and Queen Mary were due to arrive in Elland, on their journey from Halifax to Huddersfield.

36. At the north end of the bridge, overlooking the River Calder, stood Elland Hall. Once the home of the Eland family, during the 1300's. Unfortunately, during 1976, the property was demolished, due to the construction of the Elland By-Pass. However, the timbers have been preserved, with a view to eventual restoration. An added attraction to the picture is the form of travel, which was in existence during that time.

37. A section of Elland, featured from an angle of Elland Wood Bottom, Halifax Road, shows Albert Mills at Saddleworth Road. The founder of the firm being Mr. Joseph Smithies. Worsted spinning was the category of work produced here. Unfortunately, the building has now been demolished, but their are many people within Elland, who can still recall their employment within those walls.

A Quaint Bit
Elland 168

38. These steps were specially designed for the benefit of people walking from Long Wall,
down to the Saddleworth Road area. Also a valuable time-saver for employees of the
Albert Mills, situated at the foot of the steps.

39. This steam driven vehicle is present whilst works are being expedited at Elland Wood Bottom. No doubt, the result of such a task would be a smooth road, adding comfort to the highway travellers' journey.

40. Saddleworth Road, Elland. These houses were situated opposite the mill of Joseph Smithies. The view highlights the elevation of the wall, which must have taken considerable time and patience to construct.

ELLAND, FROM LONG WALL

41. This view of Long Wall shows the River Calder. The industries of the town are portrayed within this feature. Albert Mills, in the foreground, and various other manufacturing firms in the background. When Queen Victoria visited Elland, during her reign, on reaching this stage, she urged her vehicle to halt, as she admired the panoramic view.

42. Ghost stories have always been a strong point at Elland. Here, at Long Wall, the road leading to West Vale, a legend exists that the 'Long Wall Mouse' was present. The apparition, apparently, was ghostly white, and only appeared during the dark hours. The tale continues that anyone having experienced the sight, would undoubtedly undergo a great misfortune. The house on the hillside, at Hullen Edge Road, was the home of a Mr. Briggs.

43. This section of Elland, photographed from Blackley, portrays an excellent impression of the industrious area, leading from Woodman, South Lane. The amount of tall chimneys reveals the many textile mills within the area. Familiar names of such factories were Messrs. Kaye, Illingworth, Jackson Feather and Samuel Lumb, to name just a few. Following the main road, past the terraced houses of South Lane, a detached residence is outlined. Set in its own grounds, comprising of a well stocked garden, and tennis courts, the property was named 'Woodville', and was owned by the Lumb family. When finally demolished, prior to the development of Charles Street, the remaining stones were re-used and utilised in the construction of the rear elevation of those houses.

44. At Jepson Lane stood a nineteenth century building, which had previously been used as a Baptist church, and later became the Parish Hall. Misses Ashworth, of Tunbridge Wells, were the donators. Functions held there included meetings and concerts. Unfortunately, the widening of the road, at Jepson Lane, necessitated the demolition of the hall. However, plans were soon made for a replacement building. The site chosen was Westgate, and on 27th April, 1929, the doors of the Parochial Hall were officially opened.

45. The Elland Railway, opened during 1842. This means of travel must have been quite an experience for all passengers. Apparently, the seating accommodation was somewhat primitive. The carriages consisted of first, second and third class passengers. The latter category were expected to occupy compartments which resembled cattle trucks. Being without seating, they were aptly named 'Stand-up carriages'. People travelling a long distance were expected to provide their own camp style stools, or even an empty box on which to sit, throughout the journey. Pictured here are members of the staff, at Elland Railway Station.

46. A vital service available in the town was an ambulance. Journeying to hospital may not have been the most comfortable form of travel, but was certainly advantageous.

47. Solid fuel played an important role in the home and factory in those days. Prior to owning a fleet of lorries, founder members of Thompson Newsome and Company, namely John Lockwood Thompson and Joe Newsome, organised deliveries of their commodity by means of a horse and cart. The gentleman featured in the picture is Mr. Alfred Williamson.

48. South End School was officially opened on 7th January, 1878. The triangular space between Southgate and Huddersfield Road is the site which was chosen for the erection of Elland Town Hall.

Town Hall Buildings and Southgate, Elland

Another significant building is shown here, Elland Town Hall Building, and it was
for holding concerts. During June 1887, the foundation stones were laid. The
nditure totalled more than £7,000. It was an honourable occasion for Sir John Savile
ufford Abbey, near Mansfield. He was the individual, chosen to declare the official
ing of the building, on September 19th, 1888. Following the proceedings, a
eon and concert had been organised at Elland Congregational Sunday School.

50. A somewhat older picture of Town Hall Building reveals the amount of shops which were beneath the hall. Also the Town Hall Clock deserves a mention. The donation came for Mr. Lewis Mackrell, whose late father, Mr. James Mackrell, had served as Chairman of Elland Board. The official onset of the clock being in operation was on June 9th, 1909.

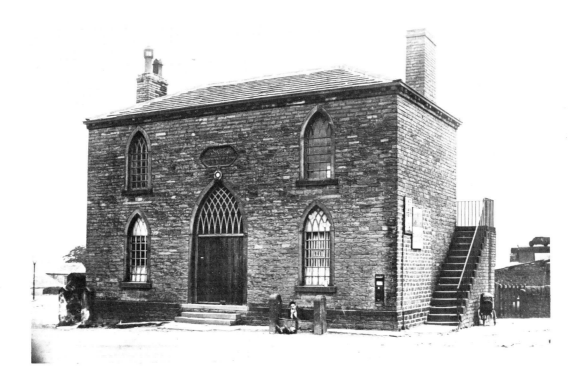

51. Situated at South End was the Elland Prison, constructed in 1821. The inscription above the door reads 'WHOSO KEEPETH THE LAW IS WISE'. The Stocks, in which the feet were fastened, played an active part in the punishment of criminals. In all probability the gentleman, featured in this picture, would be subject to the townsfolk throwing over-ripe tomatoes at him, adding to the penalty. This building was used as a prison until the 1880's, after which it became the local library, and was named the Town's Room. During 1963 the property was demolished.

52. Various characters of the town had their own meeting-place. This was known as Pinfold Parliament. In early days, prior to the area becoming the ideal situation for a gathering of gentlemen, the local cattle grazed within the grounds. When the meetings were being held at the Pinfold, seating facilities were wooden benches, and a solid fuel stove was the form of heating.

53. South House, featured above, was once the residence of Mr. Luke Crossley, a local businessman, in the dyeing trade. The property was large and the gardens were extensive. The boundary was at the Town Hall Square, close to where the Victoria Baths now stand. When the Crossley family vacated their home, the property was altered for an important purpose. Elland Urban District Council was formed during 1895, within the premises. The official opening taking place in 1896. The Chairman, chosen, was Councillor Mackrell. Parts of South House had been demolished, and a new frontage was built, with a Council Chamber on the first floor. The remainder of the property underwent conversion, and formed departments for the use of the office staff.

54. The dilapidated property, featured in this picture, is the Elizabethan Wing of South House, Southgate. The shoe, seen protruding from the front elevation of the property close by, signifies that the cobblers shop was situated there. Even nowadays, although not a family concern, footwear can be purchased from the vendor there.

The Council Offices and Market Square, Elland.

55. The Market Square and the Council Offices are illustrated here, looking towards the Southgate shopping centre. The town appears to be unusually quiet, as opposed to the normal rush and bustle of a popular area of Elland.

56. The Horse and Jockey Inn was situated beside the Ainley Woods. A well-known story about the inn involves the local Town Crier. On May 5th, 1866, he announced that an auction was to take place at the inn. Articles on offer included furniture and agricultural items. Also mentioned in the lots, was a young widow. As envisaged, a large gathering of widowers and youths were present. The auctioneer announced that the lady had already been married three times. A sovereign was the first bid, gradually progressing to £13. Then the offers slowed down, for the auctioneer declared that a reserve price had been put on the widow. Needless to say, that the sale immediately halted. The Horse and Jockey finally ceased trading on December 27th, 1933. The licensee at that time was Lily Louise Dealtry.

57. This general view of Elland shows the Horse and Jockey Inn, to the foreground. Another feature is the tall chimney of a mill at Norton Street, owned by Messrs. Casson. Directly in front of the chimney, All Saint's Church can be seen. The latter being open for public worship on November 4th, 1903.

NEW ST. ELLAND. 1912.

58. This was the inviting sight, to be seen at New Street, Elland, on June 22nd, 1911. The people made every effort to decorate the entire street with bunting, in order to celebrate the Coronation of George V, which took place at Westminster Abbey. Whenever there was a chance to decorate the thoroughfare and join in the festivities of any celebration, the Elland folks were foremost.

59. Here we see yet another form of travel, as used during the 1920's. The coach, belonging to Mr. John Harling, is seen here at the bottom of James Street. Although an excursion in the open air would be pleasant on a fine day, a fold-away canopy existed for those rainy days.

60. Various streets, lined with terraced houses, could be found at the bottom of the Ainleys, at Huddersfield Road. This particular section shows the local grocery shop. In 1910, a Mr. and Mrs. Beacock, and their son Irvine, were the owners of the corner shop. An interesting collection of hoardings, on the outer walls, portrays advertisements of various products, as available in those good old days!

61. Messrs. Dempster and Sons Limited, at Rose Mount Iron Works, Huddersfield Road, were leading craftsmen in the engineering field. Founded in 1855 by Robert Dempster, a gentleman of Scottish origin. The exact amount of skilled operatives during the early days is unknown. However, this picture offers a guide as to how business must have flourished over the years. Sadly, the Dempster company no longer exists, but Rose Mount Works can be observed when travelling from Elland to Huddersfield.

HUDDERSFIELD ROAD, ELLAND

62. This is Huddersfield Road, at the bottom side of Victoria Swimming Baths. Brook Street is the road off to the right, by the plumbers' shop. Messrs. Mellor owned a garage at the other side of Brook Street, in the foreground, beside the terraced houses. Photographed after completion of Victoria Baths, which began in 1902.

63. Dating back to the Roman era, the hillsides of Elland were renowned for their clay content. The firm of Samuel Wilkinson was founded in 1882 and situated at Blackley, Elland. Even prior to that, the Kitson family had produced pottery from those kilns. The Wilkinson company received recognition throughout the North of England, for being the largest salt glazers and pipe producers. These two employees, standing beside their lorry, are Mr. Frank Dyson and his son, Harry. It is remarkable to note the telephone number (Elland 45), displayed on the door to the vehicle.

BLACKLEY "WHIT WA

64. Religion was an important way of life, during the period which we are covering. Easter was celebrated six weeks prior to Whitsuntide. Seen here are some of the members of the Blackley Baptist Church congregation, enjoying the 'WHIT WALK'.

65. During the eighteenth century, a London haberdasher, Joseph Brooksbank, endowed a school for the needy children of Elland. In 1910, the school was constructed, the chosen site being at the top of Victoria Road. The official opening took place in September, 1911. In 1933, the school became known as Elland Grammar School. Nowadays, the school offers comprehensive education, and following the name of its founder, it is known as the 'Brooksbank School'.

66. We now look at the spectacular procession, which was organised annually by the members of Elland Carnival Committee. Captured here, in the brilliant sunshine, are dwellers of Catherine Street, welcoming the pageant.

Elland from Upper Edge 65

67. The mill of Councillor Crossley is shown above. Viewed from Dewsbury Road, Upper Edge, with the town spanning behind it. The textile trade continues within those premises nowadays, for this is the home of the well-known Gannex cloth. This picture was captured during the 1880's.

68. It is obvious, that although Elland was notorious for industry of various sources, textiles and engineering, so too, were there farmers dwelling in the outlying lands. This scene portrays how the process of harvesting was expedited.

69. Elland from Lower Edge, featuring the acres of grazing land. Examples of the industrious town can be seen in the background, notably the amount of chimneys!

70. These two girls are standing in the area of Elland Edge, the road which continued to Rastrick. To the left, at the top of the hill, a shot of the Rock Tavern can be recognised.

71. The Rock Tavern in 1911. Here a crowd at gathered, to celebrate the Coronation of King George V and Queen Mary. Sheep roasting was the main event of this scene. The victim of the barbecue, being very much to the fore.

72. Another angle of Stainland Road, showing Smith's Boot Shop, next door to the Shears Inn. At a later date, the footwear shop was rebuilt and became a two-storey building, comprising of living accommodation upstairs and the retailing of wares downstairs. The Shears Inn was formerly a sixteenth century farm building, named Lambert House.

73. Pupils of West Vale School, recorded about 1887. The little girl, third from the left on the front row, is Margaret Eastwood. The mother of a local lady, Mrs. Barraclough.

Armistice Day West Vale 1922.

74. Armistice Day at Stainland Road, West Vale. The year: 1922. Both the mill and adjacent chapel have since been demolished. People in the scene include: Mrs. Frank Wood (then Headmaster at West Vale School), Mr. Harry Whitwam, and the mother of Letty Squires.

75. Further developments appeared during the era of the tram. On the 29th May, 1914, the service was available for people wishing to travel as far as Huddersfield. This particular tram is pictured at Saddleworth Road.

76. The Stanger family, at West Vale, owned a saddlers shop. Obviously, this was a desirable line of business in the days of horse-drawn vehicles. Here we can see Mr. Owen Stanger, born in 1843 and passed away during 1921, at the age of 78. Pictured also is Mr. Nelson Stanger, a partner in the trade, who at a later date emigrated to America.